This book belongs to:

____

Made in United States
North Haven, CT
07 December 2022

28183469R00067